D0999773

All About Light and Sound

by Connie Jankowski

Science Contributor
Sally Ride Science
Science Consultants
Michael E. Kopecky, Science Educator
Jane Weir, Physicist

First hardcover edition published in 2010 by
Compass Point Books
151 Good Counsel Drive
P.O. Box 669
Mankato, MN 56002-0669

Editor: Mari Bolte
Editorial Contributor: J.M. Bedell
Designer: Heidi Thompson
Media Researcher: Svetlana Zhurkin
Production Specialist: Jane Klenk

 This book was manufactured with paper containing at least 10 percent post-consumer waste.

Library of Congress Cataloging-in-Publication Data
Jankowski, Connie.
  All about light and sound / by Connie Jankowski. — 1st hardcover ed.
    p. cm. — (Mission. Science)
  Includes index.
  ISBN 978-0-7565-4301-3 (library binding)
  1. Light—Juvenile literature. 2. Light sources—Juvenile literature.
  3. Ultraviolet radiation—Juvenile literature. 4. Sound—Juvenile
literature. I. Title. II. Series.
  QC360.J364 2009
  535—dc22   2009029356

Visit Compass Point Books, a Capstone imprint, on the Internet at *www.compasspointbooks.com*
or e-mail your request to *custserv@compasspointbooks.com*

Table of Contents

The World of Light and Sound

Think about the many things you've seen today. Maybe you noticed the sky. Was there a bird in flight? Were clouds covering the sun? Was the sky bright blue or dull gray? The truth is that you were not really seeing any of those things. You were only seeing light. Light comes to our eyes from objects as near as our nose and as far as the stars.

What do you hear now? Even in the quietest places, you can hear things. Maybe it is soft breathing. Maybe it is pages turning. Maybe an insect is buzzing or someone sneezes. When you hear those things, your ears are picking up vibrations. Your brain recognizes the vibrations as sounds.

Light and sound are two of the most important ways we know the world. They let us see and hear.

Drums create sound when the drum
▼ skin vibrates after being struck.

The Importance of Light

Without light there would be no green plants, no animals, and no human beings. Our bodies need light to make chemicals that help us fall asleep, wake up, and be happy. We need sunlight for strong bones and muscles. Without light we would be soft-boned, sleep-deprived, unhappy zombies.

Plants also need light. Their green leaves capture light and use it to make food for the plants and oxygen that animals need to breathe. Without plants there would be no food to eat and no oxygen to breathe. Most life on Earth would end.

▼ Light tells seeds when to germinate and adult plants when to flower.

The sun is Earth's main source of light and heat. The sun is a star, but much closer to us than other stars. It is not a solid or a liquid, but a gas—actually a combination of gases, mostly hydrogen and helium. The gases stay in a big ball because gravity pulls them inward. Because the sun is so huge, its gravity pushes atoms really close together, and that pressure creates heat.

The pressure and heat in the sun are so great that a powerful reaction takes place. This releases

enormous amounts of energy, which is called solar radiation. It is sent outward into the galaxy, and some of it hits Earth.

Solar radiation travels through space in waves. These waves, like water waves and sound waves, differ from each other in length (wavelength), rate (frequency), and size (amplitude).

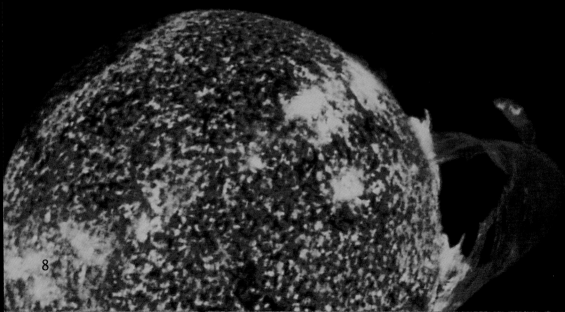

Light, like water, moves in waves. The amount of energy that a wave carries determines the color of the light.

Wavelengths of light are measured in nanometers (one-billionth of a meter). The human eye can see light wavelengths between 380 nanometers (violet) and 750 nanometers (red). These wavelenghts are called visible light. Cosmic rays, gamma rays, X-rays, ultraviolet light, and infrared light all have wavelengths or frequencies out of the range of ordinary human senses.

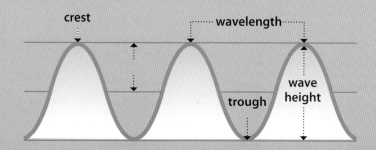

Waves of Light and Sound

Crest: The highest point of a wave

Trough: The lowest point of a wave

Wavelength: The distance from one crest or trough to the next. Different kinds of light have different wavelengths.

Wave height: The distance from the crest of a wave to the trough

Frequency: The number of times a peak or trough passes a fixed point in one second. Sound frequencies are called pitches. A chirping bird's sound is high in pitch, and a lion's roar is low-pitched.

Amplitude: The height of a wave. It shows the intensity and brightness of light, or the loudness or softness of sound.

Energy with wavelengths too short for humans to see is called bluer than blue (also known as ultraviolet light). We know these wavelengths exist because ultraviolet light, which is found in sunlight, is absorbed by our skin, causing it to tan or burn.

Energy with wavelengths too long is called redder than red (also known as infrared light). We know

How We See

Our eyes are 1 inch (25 millimeters) wide. They take in light and send information to the brain. Light enters the eye through the pupil. The pupil opens and closes to control how much light passes through to the retina. The cornea and lens focus the light before it gets to the retina. In the retina, light is changed to nerve signals and sent to the optic nerve. The optic nerve sends those signals to the brain. The brain translates the signals into images and colors.

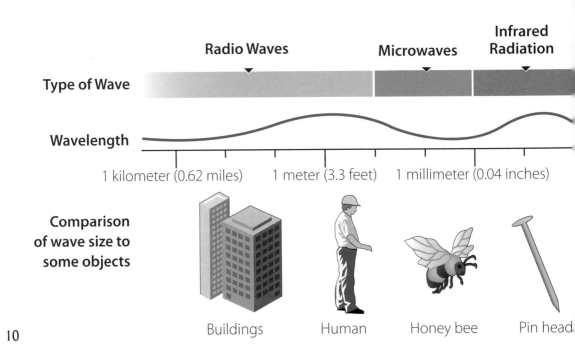

| Type of Wave | Radio Waves | Microwaves | Infrared Radiation |

Wavelength

1 kilometer (0.62 miles)   1 meter (3.3 feet)   1 millimeter (0.04 inches)

Comparison of wave size to some objects

Buildings   Human   Honey bee   Pin head

these wavelengths exist because they can be felt while sitting in front of a fire or other things that radiate heat.

The human eye can see about 7 million color variations. Some colors can cause visual fatigue, while others are more soothing. Yellow is the most tiring color for the human eye. It is also the most noticeable color because bright colors reflect more light.

Animals are on different color spectrums than humans. For example, snakes can see or sense infrared light, and that helps them find warm-blooded prey. Bees can see ultraviolet light, which reveals colors that lead them to flowers.

Light is one form of electromagnetic radiation. It shares the entire range of wavelengths with other forms, such as microwaves, X-rays, and radio waves.

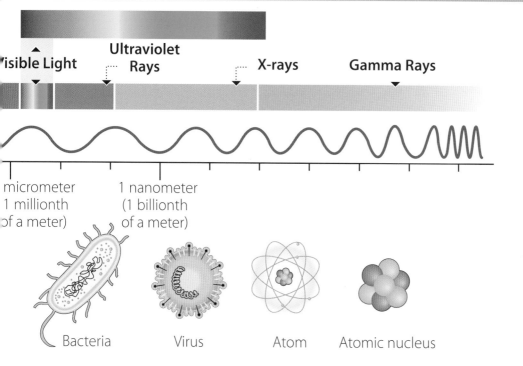

Visible Light

Ultraviolet Rays

X-rays

Gamma Rays

1 micrometer
(1 millionth
of a meter)

1 nanometer
(1 billionth
of a meter)

Bacteria

Virus

Atom

Atomic nucleus

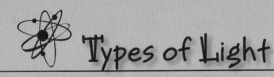
The sun produces three kinds of light—visible light, ultraviolet light, and infrared light. Visible light is the light we can see. Ultraviolet light cannot be seen because it has shorter wavelengths than visible light. Infrared light cannot be seen because it has longer wavelengths than visible light.

from red to violet—the colors of a rainbow. There is a wavelength for every color in the visible light spectrum. There are seven color ranges—reds, oranges, yellows, greens, blues, indigos, and violets. Red has the longest wavelength and violet the shortest.

Visible Light

A small part of the light spectrum is visible light. We see it as colors that range

Ultraviolet Light

Ultraviolet light is very important to humans and animals. When it hits the skin, it starts a process that

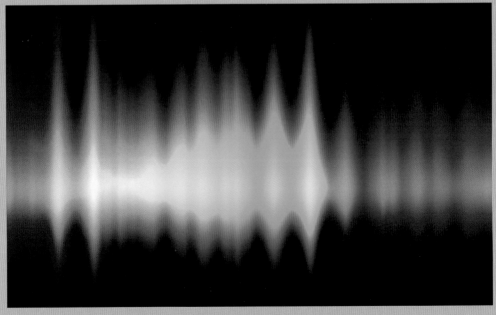

Computers can produce every color on the visible spectrum by utilizing combinations of red, green, and blue light.

makes vitamin D. We need vitamin D to build strong muscles and bones. Vitamin D is also found in eggs, fish, and cod liver oil, and it is added to most milk. Scientists think vitamin D may help protect against high blood pressure, cancer, and other diseases.

Did You Know?

Sunscreens are given Sun Protection Factor numbers based on how effective they are at protecting from UV rays. The higher the number, the higher the protection level. You should always use at least SPF 15.

It takes only 10 minutes of sunlight a day to make enough vitamin D. Too much ultraviolet light can kill healthy skin cells and cause sunburn. Sunburn can lead to wrinkles, age spots, and, in some people, skin cancer.

UV rays are strongest near the equator, at high altitudes, when the sun is highest in the sky, and in wide, open areas with no shade. Some medications can also increase the body's sensitivity to light. Your risk of UV exposure doesn't decrease on cloudy days—since UV is a type of invisible radiation and not visible light, it can shine through clouds.

Although many people use tanning beds in the belief that they will get a "base" tan, the UV rays of a tanning bed do not protect the skin against future sunburns.

Infrared Light

Infrared light from the sun provides about half of Earth's heat. The other heat source is Earth's molten core. Infrared light is what you feel when you sit outside in the sun. Strong infrared light and long outdoor exposure should be avoided. They can damage your vision.

Researchers have found many ways to use infrared light. The military uses it to help soldiers see at night and to track flying missiles and aircraft. Astronomers use it with their telescopes to see through regions in space.

Night vision is just one ➡ way humans can utilize infrared light.

Optics

Optics is the branch of science that examines the behaviors and properties of light. Scientists have used their understanding of optics to invent many important devices. Eyeglasses help us see near and far. Microscopes allow us to study very tiny objects. Telescopes let us study objects that are far away. Optics is used in making binoculars, magnifying glasses, and cameras.

When light waves hit an object, some waves are reflected, and some are absorbed. The color of the object depends on which waves are reflected and which are taken in.

Grass looks green to you because green light waves are being reflected and captured by your eye. All the other waves are absorbed and can't be seen. An apple looks red because red light waves are reflected, and all the others are absorbed.

Color Blindness

Inside the eye's retina are cells shaped like cones and rods. The cone cells help us see in bright light, and the rod cells help us see at night. There are millions of these cells in every eye. Cone cells help us tell colors apart. Some cone cells react to short wavelengths (blues), some to medium wavelengths (greens), and others to long wavelengths (reds).

If someone is born without these cells, or they are damaged, then that person sees colors differently. The most common color blindness is in not seeing reds or greens properly. Not seeing blues is very rare. Color blindness is usually inherited, and it usually happens to males.

Another thing that can happen to light is refraction. Refraction means bending or changing direction. When light passes from air into water, it slows and bends. You can see this if you put a straw into a glass of water. At the surface of the water, the straw will seem to be cut in half.

A beautiful example of refraction is a rainbow. Light from the sun hits water molecules in the air. The waves slow and bend. Each wave bends at a slightly different angle and is separated from the others. When this happens, we see a rainbow and all the colors of the visible light spectrum.

As the light passes through the glass, it slows down. When the light passes through the water, you can see the straw appears to be cut in half.

Refracted light has many uses. It can make objects appear closer, so we use it for binoculars, periscopes, and telescopes. Fiber optic cables use refraction to transmit images for television and the Internet. Diamonds are carefully cut so that when light hits them, it refracts and makes them sparkle.

Did You Know?

Light travels through a diamond at less than half the speed of light.

Nature's Light

Some animals, plants, and minerals give off light, and you can see them in the dark. The light appears when certain chemicals are combined. In living organisms, this is called bioluminescence. Most bioluminescence happens in the oceans, not in freshwater.

Fluorescence and phosphorescence, known as cold light, are kinds of light that emit no heat. Both happen when a light-emitting object is exposed to energy. Atoms are excited and create light that can be seen through a microscope, by using certain filters, or by the eye. Fluorescent light disappears when the energy source is removed, but phosphorescent light continues after the energy source is removed.

Glowworms, lightning bugs, and a fungus called foxfire can light up the night. Underwater light makers include certain kinds of jellyfish, squid, shrimp, and fish. Deep underground are minerals that glow in the dark.

Jellyfish glow under ultraviolet light. In 2008 chemists found a way to isolate the protein that causes the glow.

Artificial Light

There are ways to have light without the sun. Until the discovery of electricity, people used firelight, gas and oil lanterns, and candles to see at night. Today we have electricity and use lightbulbs. There are several kinds of bulbs.

Incandescent: Electricity heats a filament in the bulb and makes it glow. These bulbs produce a steady, warm light. They last from 700 to 1,000 hours.

Halogen: Electricity is passed through a filament enclosed in a tube of halogen gas. These bulbs use less power and have a longer life than incandescent bulbs. But they cost more, burn hotter, and can be a fire hazard.

Fluorescent: Electricity passes through a tube filled with argon and mercury. These bulbs last between 10,000 and 20,000 hours. They use much less power than regular bulbs and produce little heat. But they contain mercury, which can harm the environment, and must be recycled.

Light-emitting diodes: These lights use small amounts of electricity and have no filament. They last a long time, but they aren't as bright as other bulbs. LEDs are a new technology, and they are expected to improve in the coming years.

Humans can live without sound, but it's hard. Sound surrounds us all the time. We hear our first sounds before we are born. In the womb, a baby can hear music, voices, and the beating of its mother's heart. As we grow, we use sound to learn languages and to discover our world.

Most animals need sound, too. If an animal in the wild could not hear, it probably would die. It could not hear its prey or its predators. It probably would starve or become another animal's meal. Some animals use sound to communicate with each other, while others use it to find their way in the dark.

Scientific experiments suggest that plants react to sound. They sense the vibrations, and that seems to stimulate growth. There is no proof that playing music or singing to a plant will make it grow faster, but it can't hurt. So go ahead and sing to your favorite tree.

Our Singing Sun

The sun vibrates, creating sounds, but it is more than 93 million miles (150 million kilometers) away from Earth and surrounded by the vacuum of space. Since sound cannot travel through a vacuum, we can't hear the sun's music. But scientists have detected the vibrations.

The sun pulses in and out in a complex pattern, creating sound waves. Using an instrument on a spacecraft, astronomers have recorded the waves. Their frequency is too low for the human ear to hear. So scientists took 40 days' worth of sun vibrations and compressed them into a few seconds. Then they increased their speed 42,000 times. That made it possible for the sounds to be heard.

Like light, sound is energy and it travels in waves. Sound happens when molecules in the air are moved. When a dog barks, air molecules jump and then bang into other molecules, causing a chain reaction. The chain reaction makes sound waves that are picked up by our ears. Our ears transfer the sound to our brains, and our brains think, "Aha! I recognize that sound. It's a dog barking."

Not all sound waves are alike. The differences let us hear various sounds.

Scientists have discovered that, like light, sounds and sound waves differ in wavelength, amplitude, and frequency.

As with light, the wavelength refers to the distance between one peak and the next.

Amplitude is the height of the sound wave and relates to the loudness or softness of a sound. When a wave is high, the sound is loud and the amplitude is large. When a wave is low, the amplitude is small and the sound is soft.

We can tell sounds apart by the vibrations they make.

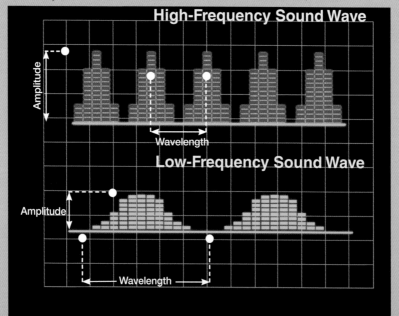

High-Frequency Sound Wave

Amplitude

Wavelength

Low-Frequency Sound Wave

Amplitude

Wavelength

The frequency of sound relates to speed. The number of cycles per second that waves pass a given location is the frequency. The brain understands the frequency as pitch. Fast vibrations cause high pitch, and slower vibrations make lower-pitched sounds.

Did You Know?

Sound waves bounce off the surface of the sun and also travel deep into its center core. Because of this movement, the sun is full of musical notes. It actually rings like a bell.

The Doppler Effect

As you know, the frequency of a sound wave is called pitch. The pitch (highness or lowness) of a sound seems to change as the source of the sound moves closer or farther away. This is called the Doppler effect.

Stand on the sidewalk and listen to the siren of a fire truck. As the truck moves closer, the sound waves are squeezed together. The gap between waves gets smaller, so the pitch increases. The sound of the siren seems to get higher. As the fire truck moves away, the sound waves expand and the pitch decreases. The sound seems to get lower. The firefighters on the truck don't hear this change because they're moving at the same speed as the source of the sound.

Even if you close your eyes, you will know whether the fire truck is moving toward you or away from you by the change in pitch. If you measure the rate of the change, you can even estimate the truck's speed.

There wasn't really a change in the frequency of the sound coming from the siren. That remains constant. But your ears heard it as a change because of the squeezing and expanding of the waves—the Doppler effect.

The Speed of Sound

How fast sound waves move depends on what they are traveling through. Through the air, sound travels about 1,115 feet (340 meters) per second at sea level. The speed changes if the sound waves are moving through water or a solid object.

Several things affect the speed of sound: elasticity, temperature, vacuum, and inertia.

original form. Steel has high elasticity, water has less, and gases have the least. Steel molecules strongly attract each other. Water molecules have a weaker attraction, and gas molecules have the weakest. The greater the molecular attraction in an object, the faster sound can travel through it. Sound moves faster through solids than through liquids, and faster through liquids than through gases.

Elasticity

Elasticity is an object's ability to return to its

▲ A sonic boom cloud sometimes forms when a jet breaks the sound barrier.

Sonic Boom

Have you ever heard a big boom and wondered what made it? It could have been an airplane flying faster than the speed of sound. This is called supersonic flight, and it causes a sonic boom. As the airplane nears the speed of sound, the air in front of it begins to pile up. You hear a boom when the shock wave, a sudden change in air pressure, hits your ear.

If you stand on the ground and the plane passes overhead at Mach 1 (the speed of sound), you will hear a boom as it passes. If the plane is moving faster than the speed of sound, the boom will be delayed and is heard after the plane passes.

Temperature

Warm molecules vibrate faster, and sound waves pass through them more quickly. Cold molecules vibrate slowly, and sound waves travel more slowly. The speed of sound is less at the icy North Pole than at the warm, tropical areas near the equator.

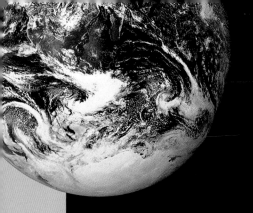

Silent Space

**If you travel about 78 miles
(126 km) above Earth, you will
be in outer space. It is a vacuum,
but it is not completely empty.
Gas and dust are out there.
Scientists estimate there are
several hundred molecules per
cubic meter. All together, it's a
lot. But it's still not enough to
transmit sound.**

Vacuum

Sound can't go through
a vacuum. A vacuum is a
space with little or nothing
in it. Since sound happens
when molecules bounce
off each other, and there
are few or no molecules in
a vacuum, there can be no
sound. If you put a ringing
bell into a jar and remove
all the air, the bell will keep
ringing. But you won't be
able to hear it, since there
aren't enough molecules to
create a sound wave.

Inertia

Inertia also affects the speed
of sound. Inertia is an object's
tendency to keep doing what
it's doing. If it is still, inertia
means it will stay there until
something moves it. If the
object is moving, it will keep
moving at the same speed,
and in the same direction,
unless something changes
its motion. If sound travels
through molecules that
have a lot of inertia—the
molecules react slowly to
each other—its speed is
lower. If the molecules have
less inertia and react faster,
the sound's speed increases.
Sound travels nearly three
times as fast in helium as it
does in air because helium
molecules react faster than
air molecules.

Did You Know?

**The word *inertia* comes from
the Latin word *iners*, which
means idle or lazy.**

Ears

The human ear has three sections. The outer ear collects sound waves and funnels them into the ear canal. The outer ear also helps to identify the direction from which a sound is coming.

The middle ear holds the eardrum, which vibrates with the sound waves, and transfers them to three tiny bones. These bones are called the hammer, the anvil, and the stirrup. The hammer, anvil, and stirrup repeat the eardrum vibrations and transfer them to the cochlea.

The cochlea is in the inner ear. It is filled with fluid and is spiral-shaped. It is in the cochlea that sound vibrations are changed to electrical impulses and sent along a nerve to the brain. The brain interprets the impulses and recognizes the thousands of sounds we hear each day.

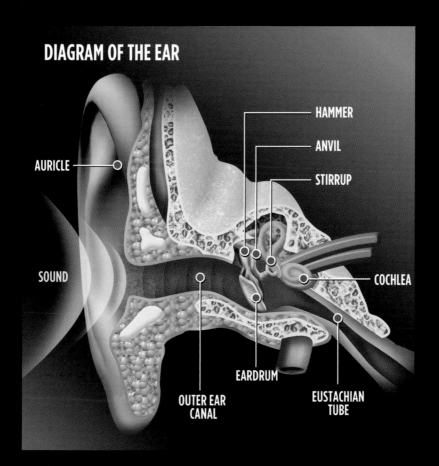

DIAGRAM OF THE EAR

HAMMER

ANVIL

AURICLE

STIRRUP

SOUND

COCHLEA

EARDRUM

OUTER EAR CANAL

EUSTACHIAN TUBE

Vibrations

The normal human ear can pick up sounds that have frequencies of 20 to 20,000 vibrations per second.

Sounds below 20 vibrations per second are called subsonic. Those above 20,000 are called ultrasonic.

Whose Ear Is Best?

Did you know that dogs hear better than cats, and both of them hear most sounds better than we do? What animals can hear is related to what they need to hear in order to survive in the wild.

	LOW FREQUENCY (vibrations per second)	HIGH FREQUENCY (vibrations per second)
Humans	20	20,000
Cats	100	32,000
Dogs	40	46,000
Bats	1,000	150,000
Elephants	16	12,000
Seals and sea lions	200	55,000
Whales and dolphins	70	150,000

Sound happens when molecules bounce around. Humans and animals make these molecules bounce in different ways.

People make sounds using their larynx. The larynx is in the neck and is made of two pieces of strong elastic tissue called cartilage. We need a larynx to breathe, swallow, and speak. Two pieces of tissue, called the vocal cords, stretch across the larynx. The cords open and close to allow air and food to enter the body. As the muscles around the larynx relax or tighten, and we pull air in or push air out, the vocal cords vibrate. The vibrations are sounds—speaking, singing, and everything else our voices can do.

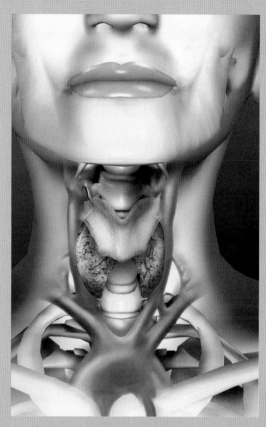

The larynx is also called the voice box.

Animal Sounds

Most mammals have a voice box, too. Theirs don't look like ours, but they do the same job. Some animals make sounds in other ways. Dolphins click and whistle through their blowholes. A bee's rapidly flapping wings make a buzzing sound. Crickets chirp by rubbing their wings together. And frogs croak by quickly releasing air from their lungs.

27

Instruments

Musical instruments can make a variety of sounds. Percussion instruments, such as drums and xylophones, make sounds when they are struck. String instruments, such as violins and guitars, make sounds when their strings vibrate. That happens when a bow slides across violin strings or a pick plucks guitar strings.

Woodwind instruments, such as flutes, clarinets, and saxophones, make sounds when air is blown through the mouthpiece, making reeds inside vibrate. Brass instruments, such as trumpets, trombones, and french horns, rely on the player's lips to vibrate the air, which flows through the instrument.

The many sounds produced by instruments in an orchestra blend to make one pleasing effect.

Sound vibrations serve many purposes. Some sounds are simply for pleasure. For example, we enjoy listening to a radio, a concert, or a movie soundtrack. Other sounds serve as cautions and warnings. Thunder, wind, and crashing waves give messages about harsh weather. Engine vibrations reveal the working conditions of a car or truck. A loud sound warns that danger may be near.

Doctors use sound to capture pictures inside the body. This technique is called ultrasound imaging. Ultrasound images can help diagnose health problems. A doctor can also use them to see how a baby is developing before it is born.

Sonar is another way to use sound to create images. Sound waves bounce off objects, and their images appear on a display screen. Scientists use sonar to map the floor of the ocean and to locate hidden objects. It is also used to navigate and to track ships and submarines.

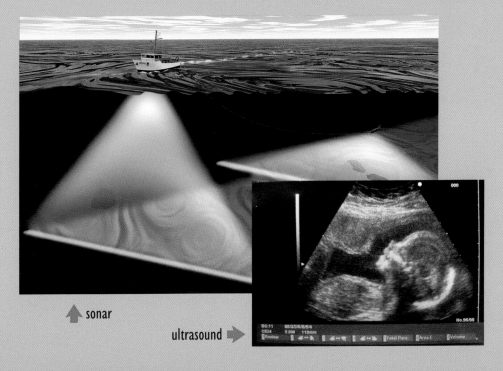

sonar

ultrasound

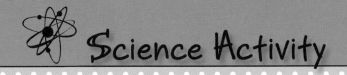

Periscopes have been used for many years. Sailors on submarines use them to see above water. Doctors use a type of periscope to look inside the body. Using the principles of light from this book, you can make your own periscope.

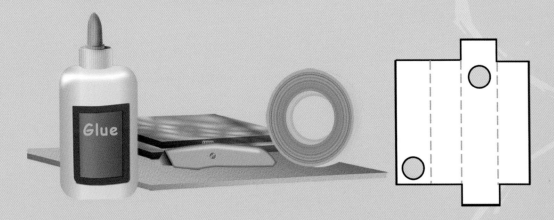

Materials

- 2 small mirrors

- Stiff cardboard

- Craft knife (use only with adult help)

- Glue (strong enough to support a mirror)

- Masking tape or wide clear tape

Procedure

1   Build the body of your periscope from cardboard. Follow the pattern shown on this page to create a hollow shaft to support your mirrors. Note the position of the tabs. Trace and cut the pattern from the cardboard. Take care when cutting the round holes.

2 Fold the cardboard along the
dotted lines on the pattern. It may
help to score the folds with a craft
knife to make the bending easier.

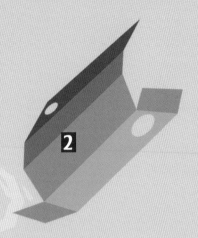

3 Assemble the shaft (the box). Fold
the sides as shown. Tape the long
side closed to form a rectangular
tube with flaps. Leave the top and
bottom flaps open. Lay the box on
its back with the top hole on your
right side.

4 Attach a strip of tape to the edge of a mirror. Slide
the mirror into the box end with the reflecting side up.
(You should be looking into the mirror when you look
into the hole.) Tape or glue the mirror in place.

5 Turn the box end up, with the
mirror at the top. Push the mirror
to angle it at 45 degrees. Be sure
you can close the box lid over the
mirror. Keep the mirror's angle by
using tape to hold it in place.

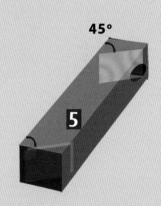

6 Turn the box and repeat
the procedure to install the
second mirror. Enjoy using
your periscope.

Alhazen (965–1040)
Arab scientist and mathematician who accurately described light rays and their role in making vision possible; he is sometimes called the founder of optics

Aristotle (384–322 B.C.)
Greek philosopher who said that moving air carries sound

Robert Boyle (1627–1691)
Irish chemist and physicist who showed that sound does not travel through a vacuum

Jacqueline Cochran (1906–1980)
Female aviator who was the first woman to fly a jet across the ocean, to fly a bomber across the Atlantic, and to break the sound barrier

Thomas A. Edison (1847–1931)
American inventor and businessman who invented the first practical phonograph and perfected the first incandescent lightbulb

Albert Einstein (1879–1955)
German-born American theoretical physicist and one of the greatest scientists in history; best known for his theories of relativity, especially one describing the relationship between mass and energy using the formula $E = mc^2$

Lene Hau (1959–   )
Danish physicist who was able to slow the speed of light and stop light for a split second

Christiaan Huygens (1629–1695)
Dutch physicist who proposed the theory that light travels in waves

Ernst Mach (1838–1916)
Austrian physicist who discovered that airflow is disturbed at the speed of sound; Mach numbers, which show how fast something is moving compared with the speed of sound, were named for him

Albert A. Michelson (1852–1931)
American physicist who showed that the speed of light is constant; his work laid the foundation for Albert Einstein's theories of relativity; in 1907 he became the first American to win a Nobel Prize in science when he received the Nobel Prize in physics

Edward Morley (1838–1923)
American chemist and physicist who, along with Albert Michelson, developed the interferometer to show that the velocity of light is a constant

Sir Isaac Newton (1643–1727)
English scientist who found that white light contains all colors, which can be separated using a prism; his work laid the foundation for the study of optics

Lord Rayleigh (1842–1919)
British physicist who studied color vision and sound and described important principles of acoustics

Ole Römer (1644–1710)
Danish astronomer who proved that there is a limit to the speed of light

Thomas Young (1773–1829)
English physicist who demonstrated that light moves in waves and whose work was the foundation for the development of prescription eyeglasses

Light and Sound Through Time

c. 700 B.C.	Pythagoras incorrectly explains vision by saying rays go from the eye to an object; he also experiments with vibrating strings used to make music
c. 350 B.C.	Greek philosopher Aristotle correctly says sound is carried by moving air
c. 1030s A.D.	Arab scientist Alhazen explains vision correctly by saying light rays reflect from objects and enter the eye
early 1600s	Italian physicist Galileo tries without success to measure the speed of light; he also studies vibrations and sound pitch and frequency
17th century	French scientist Pierre Gassendi makes the first recorded attempt to measure the speed of sound in air
1704	Isaac Newton argues that light is made of a stream of particles, which he called corpuscles; scientists today believe light has properties of both waves and particles
1826	Swiss physicist Daniel Colladon makes the first measurement of the speed of sound in water
1842	Austrian physicist Christian Doppler shows that sound waves from a source moving toward the listener seem to rise in frequency, and lower when the source is going away; this is known as the Doppler effect
1864	British physicist James Clerk Maxwell discovers that light is related to electricity and magnetism

1877	American inventor Thomas Edison creates the phonograph, the first device that can record and reproduce sounds
1878	British physicist Lord Rayleigh describes important principles of acoustics, the study of sound properties
1905	German-born physicist Albert Einstein proposes that light consists of "chunks" (later called photons); he also offers his special theory of relativity, which showed that the speed of light is constant and cannot be exceeded, now a basic principle of physics
1920	Commercial radio station 8MK in Detroit, Michigan, begins regular broadcasting; station KDKA in Pittsburgh, Pennsylvania, broadcasts the results of the 1920 presidential election
1926	American physicist Albert Michelson accurately measures the speed of light
1947	Chuck Yeager becomes the first person to break the sound barrier
1950s	The U.S. Navy begins building a global underwater sound monitoring system to detect and track Soviet ships and submarines; it is later used for tracking whales and for other scientific purposes
1953	Jacqueline Cochran becomes the first woman to break the sound barrier
1982	Compact discs that can store sound are sold for the first time, in Europe and Japan; they appear in the United States in 1983

1990	The Hubble Space Telescope, designed to peer deep into space using optical and infrared observation equipment, is placed in orbit; it eventually showed the formation of galaxies soon after the explosive birth of the universe
1996	One trillion bits of data per second are transmitted through fiber-optic cables
1999	Danish scientist Lene Hau freezes atoms, slowing the speed of light to 37 miles (60 kilometers) per hour.
2008	American scientists Martin Chalfie and Robert Tsien and Japanese scientist Osamu Shimomura win the Nobel Prize in chemistry for isolating the protein in jellyfish that glows green when exposed to ultraviolet light
2009	U.S. astronauts make the last of several repair visits to the Hubble Space Telescope, which is expected to function until 2014

Glossary

amplitude—distance from the midpoint of a wave to its crest; a measure of wave strength

fiber optic—made of transparent glass or plastic fibers that can transmit light

filament—thread or wire in a lightbulb that glows when electricity goes through it

frequency—rate at which an event occurs, such as the number of wave crests that pass a fixed point each second

refraction—change in the direction of light or sound waves when they enter a new medium at an angle

sonar—device that measures the distance to an object by bouncing sound waves off of it and timing their return

sonic boom—noise made by sound waves when their source, such as an airplane, travels faster than the speed of sound

sound waves—form of sound energy when it passes through something, such as air

spectrum—entire range of something, such as white light, which contains all colors

speed of light—speed at which light travels in empty space, about 186,000 miles (299,460 kilometers) per second

speed of sound—speed at which sound travels, about 760 miles (1,224 km) per hour at sea level

ultrasound imaging—process that uses high-frequency sound to create images of the inside of an object, such as a human body

vibrations—repeated back-and-forth motions

wavelength—distance from one wave crest to the next

waves—energy moving through a medium, such as water or air

white light—combination of all light wavelengths that the brain perceives as colorless, such as sunlight

Allday, Jonathan. *Light and Sound*. New York: Oxford University Press, 2002.

Bang, Molly. *My Light*. New York: Blue Sky Press, 2004.

Burgan, Michael. *Thomas Alva Edison: Great American Inventor*. Minneapolis: Compass Point Books, 2007.

Solway, Andrew. *Exploring Sound, Light, and Radiation*. New York: Rosen Central, 2008.

Stille, Darlene R. *Waves: Energy on the Move*. Minneapolis: Compass Point Books, 2006.

Internet Sites

FactHound offers a safe, fun way to find Internet sites related to this book. All of the sites on FactHound have been researched by our staff.

Here's all you do:
  Visit *www.facthound.com*
FactHound will fetch the best sites for you!

Index

Connie Jankowski

Connie Jankowski is a seasoned journalist, marketing expert, public relations consultant, and teacher. Her education includes a Bachelor of Arts from the University of Pittsburgh and graduate study at Pitt. She has worked in publishing, public relations, and marketing for the past 25 years. She is the author of 11 books and hundreds of magazine articles.

Image Credits